SCIENCE EXPERIMENTS
Electricity and Static Force

Om Books International

Om Books International

Reprinted in 2025

Corporate & Editorial Office
A-12, Sector 64, Noida 201 301
Uttar Pradesh, India
Phone: +91 120 477 4100
Email: editorial@ombooks.com
Website: www.ombooksinternational.com

Sales Office
107, Ansari Road, Darya Ganj
New Delhi 110 002, India
Phone: +91 11 4000 9000
Email: sales@ombooks.com
Website: www.ombooks.com

ISBN: 978-93-52763-89-4

Printed in India

10 9 8 7 6 5 4 3

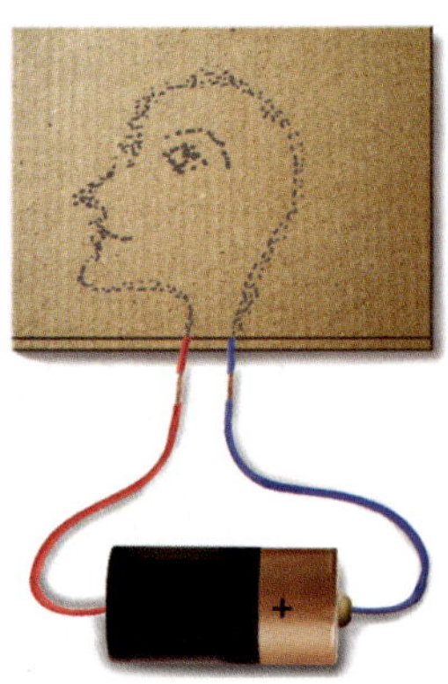

CONTENTS

Duration of Experiment	Difficulty Level	Adult Supervision
5 mins		
This icon indicates approximately how long the experiment will take, including the set-up time.	The black bars in this icon indicate level of difficulty in doing this experiment with one icon depicting the least level of difficulty.	This icon indicates that parental supervision is required. Always have an adult beside you.

NOTE: All activities and experiments described in this book should be ideally performed with adult supervision. Parents and guardians are advised to oversee the children and assist them with any difficult or potentially harmful tools. Common sense and discretion are advised. The publisher does not assume any responsibility for any injuries or damages arising from any activities.

Tsp - teaspoon Tbsp - tablespoon ml - millilitre l - litre gm - gram 1 cup - 250 millilitre cm - centimetre

Ice Tray Battery

Duration of Experiment: 10 mins.

Difficulty Level:

What you need:

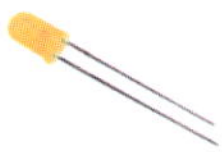

5mm 1 LED light

1 Ice tray

Distilled white vinegar

5 pieces of copper wire

5 galvanised nails

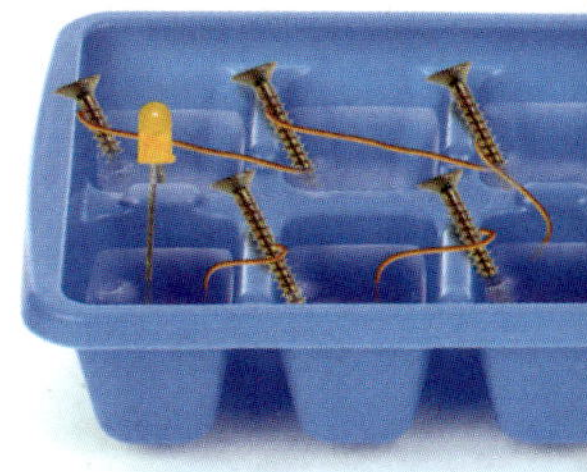

What to do:

Step 1. Wrap all the nails with pieces of copper wire, leaving a section extending below the head of the nails.

Step 2. Fill six wells of an ice tray with distilled white vinegar. Insert each nail into a vinegar well, placing the wire in the next well.

Step 3. Place the "legs" of an LED light as shown. If it doesn't light, flip the legs.

What just happened?

Batteries comprise of two different metals. When they are suspended in an acidic solution, the current flows out of the wire and into the nail.

Electric Slime

Duration of Experiment: 20 mins.

Difficulty Level:

What you need:

3 tbsps cornflour

Spoon

Balloon

Cup

3 tbsps vegetable oil

What to do:

Step 1. Mix the vegetable oil and the cornflour in the cup. The consistency should be similar to that of thick cream.

Step 2. Blow the balloon and rub it against your hair.

Step 3. Put a bit of the mixture in the spoon and move it towards the balloon.

You will notice that the mixture becomes thick and 'moves towards' the balloon.

What just happened?

Rubbing the balloon against your hair gives it a positive charge. The starch molecules in the cornflour are attracted to the balloon as a result.

Conductor of Electricity

Duration of Experiment: 10 mins.

Difficulty Level:

What you need:

Clip

Flashlight bulb

Battery

Coin

Tape

Scissors

Aluminium foil

What to do:

Step 1. Cut the aluminium foil to make two 60 cm strips.

Step 2. Tape one end of both strips to the battery.
Wrap the other end around the base of the bulb.

Step 3. Use the clip to hold it in place.

Step 4. Now, touch the base of the bulb to the coin. See the bulb light up!

What just happened?

Some materials allow electricity to pass through them easily and some do not. The coin completes the circuit by allowing electricity to pass through it.

Simple Motor

Duration of Experiment: 20 mins.

Difficulty Level:

What you need:

Copper wire

3 neodymium magnets

Battery

What to do:

Step 1. Twist the wire into a shape that can balance on the top of the battery as well as around the magnets.

Step 2. Arrange the objects as shown in the image.

Step 3. Watch the wire rotate.

What just happened?

Charge runs through the wire. The north and south poles of the magnet attract and repel the charge continuously, causing the wire to spin.

Coin Power

Duration of Experiment: 15 mins.

Difficulty Level:

What you need:

Lemon

Tissue strips

Bowl

Coins – copper and stainless steel

What to do:

Step 1. Squeeze the lemon into the bowl. Dip the tissue strips in it.

Step 3. Make a tower of alternating copper and non-copper coins separated by the lemon soaked strips, until your tower reaches a total of 10 coins.

Step 4. Wet your first finger and thumb. You will feel a mild shock!

What just happened?

The two types of coins have different electrical charges. The lemon acts as an acid and conducts this electricity. By stacking the coins on top of each other, the charge increased till it was enough to give you a shock.

Dead or Alive?

Duration of Experiment: 1 hour

Difficulty Level:

What you need:

Pin

Salt

Dead dry cell

Cloth

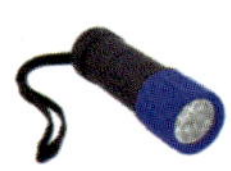

Flashlight

Water

Jar

What to do:

Step 1. Make several holes in the top of the dead dry cell.

Step 2. Dissolve a packet of salt in the large jar of water.

Step 3. Place the cell in the jar.

Step 4. After an hour, take it out. Dry it with the cloth.

Step 5. Put it in a flashlight and watch the bulb light up.

What just happened?

When a battery dies, the liquid in the battery called 'electrolyte' dries up. Salt water is a substitute for the electrolyte. So when the battery soaks in the salt, it replaces the electrolyte and revives the battery.

Sticky Glasses

Duration of Experiment: 5 mins.

Difficulty Level:

What you need:

2 plastic glasses

Paper towel

Hot water

What to do:

Step 1. Wet the paper towel with the hot water, but don't crumple it.

Step 2. Fill one of the plastic glasses with hot water and pour it out.

Step 3. Lay the paper on top of this glass.

Step 4. Pour some water into the other glass and pour it out.

Step 5. Turn this glass over and put it on top of the paper towel.

Step 6. Hold it there for 30 seconds and pick it up.

You will find that both glasses are stuck to each other.

SCIENCE AROUND US

What is heat energy?
Heat energy is the term used to describe the level of activity in the molecules of an object. The Sun is the primary source of heat energy in our solar system.

What just happened?

When you pour the hot water into the glasses, it heats the air inside, which expands. Once the air starts cooling, the pressure reduces, but new air cannot enter the glasses because they are stuck together. The pressure from the air outside keeps the glasses firmly stuck to each other.

Glowing Lead

Duration of Experiment: 30 mins.

Difficulty Level:

What you need:

8 D-sized batteries

Alligator clips

Electric tape

Glass jar

Aluminium plate

0.5 mm pencil lead

Cardboard tube

What to do:

Step 1. Tape the D-sized batteries together, with the positive end of one battery touching the negative end of the other.

Step 2. Cut the tube to a height that fits comfortably in the glass jar.

Step 3. Tape one positive and one negative alligator clip to one end of the tube.

Step 4. Carefully place a mechanical pencil lead between the two alligator clips.

Step 5. Place the glass jar over the top of the tube stand and place the plate under it, as shown.

Step 6. Touch the other ends of the alligator clips to the ends of the battery.

Step 7. In a moment, the pencil lead begins to glow.

What just happened?

You completed the circuit by touching the ends of the alligator clips to the battery. This flow of electricity heats the pencil lead to an incredible temperature, which makes it glow and let out smoke.

Electric Telegraph

Duration of Experiment: 10 mins.

Difficulty Level:

What you need:

30 ft insulated wire

3-volt light bulb

6-volt lantern battery

What to do:

Step 1. Build a long circuit by connecting the terminals of a bulb and the terminals of the battery cell with the wire.

Step 2. Keep the bulb and battery in different rooms.

Step 3. Disconnect one terminal of the battery and reconnect it. Send short or long bursts of light according to any code that you and your friends develop.

Step 4. You can now send a message to your friend in another room just like a telegraph message!

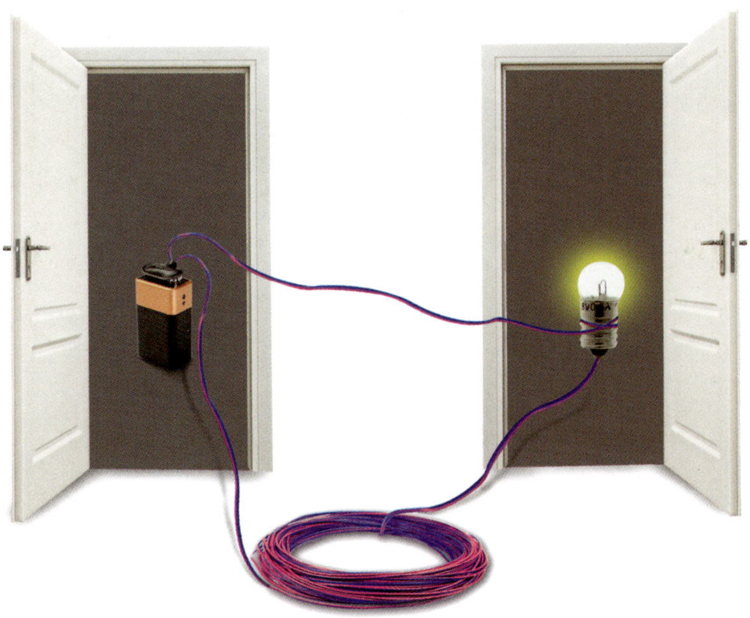

What just happened?

When the circuit is connected the lightbulb switches on. The length of time of the connection signals the amount of time the bulb will be lit. This concept is used to build the codes.

Lighten Up!

Duration of Experiment: 20 mins.

Difficulty Level:

What you need:

Paper cutter

Battery

Flashlight bulb

Tape

5 inch wire

What to do:

Step 1. Scrape the insulation off both ends of the wire.

Step 2. Curl one end of the wire tightly around the grooves at the base of the bulb.

Step 3. Shape the other end into a coil.

Step 4. Tape the coil to the bottom of a dry cell.

Step 5. Tape the rest of the wire to the cell such that the base of the bulb can touch the positive terminal of the battery.

SCIENCE AROUND US

How do electric switches work?

Switches work in a similar manner to the circuits you just made. When the switch is in an 'on' position, it completes the circuit. That is how electrons flow and whatever appliance you are switching 'on' works. On the other hand, in an 'off' position, the circuit is broken. This causes the flow of electrons to stop and the appliance to stop working.

What just happened?

By connecting the positive and negative terminals of the battery, you completed the circuit, causing electricity to flow. This electric power lit up the bulb.

Bending Water

Duration of Experiment: 10 mins.

Difficulty Level:

What you need:

Plastic comb

Narrow stream of water from a tap

What to do:

Step 1. Turn on the water so it falls from the tap in a narrow stream.

Step 2. Run the comb through your hair around 10 times.

Step 3. Slowly, move the comb towards the water (without touching it).

Step 4. You will see the water 'bend'.

What just happened?

The static electricity you built up by combing your hair attracts the stream of water, bending it towards or away from the comb!

Can Follower

Duration of Experiment: 20 mins.

Difficulty Level:

What you need:

Woollen fabric

Aluminium can

Inflated balloon

What to do:

Step 1. Rub the balloon against the woollen fabric.

Step 2. Put the aluminium can on its side on a table.

Step 3. Hold the balloon close to the can and watch as the can rolls towards it.

Step 4. Slowly use the balloon to lead the can.

What just happened?

Rubbing the balloon against the woollen fabric creates static electricity. This involves negatively charged particles (electrons) moving from the wool to the balloon. The aluminium can, which is neutral, is drawn to the negatively charged balloon.

Static Magic

Duration of Experiment: 30 mins.

Difficulty Level:

What you need:

Styrofoam ball

Plastic straw

Woollen fabric

What to do:

Step 1. Wrap the piece of fabric around the plastic straw and rub it 20 times.

Step 2. Place the now magic straw above the foam ball and watch the ball mysteriously jump up to the straw.

What just happened?

When the straw is rubbed with the fabric it gets charged. This gives it the power to attract things like the styrofoam ball.

Swinging Cereal

Duration of Experiment: 10 mins.

Difficulty Level:

What you need:

Comb

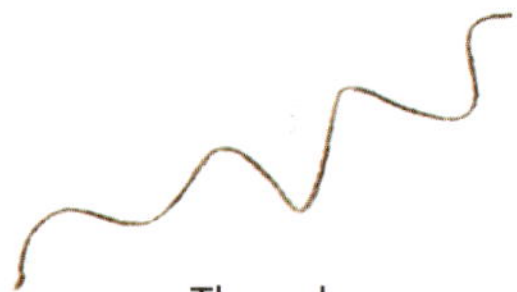
Thread

Doorknob

Small pieces of dry cereal

What to do:

Step 1. Tie a piece of cereal to one end of a string.
Step 2. Hang the string from a metal doorknob.
Step 3. Comb your hair briskly with a dry comb around 20 times.
Step 4. Now bring the comb close to the cereal. It will swing to touch the comb.
Step 5. Wait for a few seconds till it jumps away.
Step 6. Now every time you try to touch it, it will move away.
Step 7. You can control the cereal in this way, just like a remote control car!

What just happened?

When you combed your hair, the comb got negatively charged. Being neutral, the cereal jumped towards the comb. As soon as this happened, negative electrons got transferred from the comb to the cereal. Once this happened, both objects had a negative charge and repelled each other.

SCIENCE AROUND US

Photocopy machines use static electricity

It's true! In copy machines more ink gets attracted to darker areas because of static. Copy machines use the charge to apply ink only in the areas where the paper to be copied is darker and not where the paper is white.

Shock Yourself

Duration of Experiment: 20 mins.

Difficulty Level:

What you need:

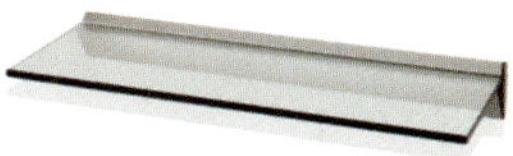

Glass slab

Piece of fur

Tap

What to do:

Step 1. On a dry day, place the glass slab on the floor.

Step 2. Stand on the slab. Have your friend rub your back with the fur several times.

Step 3. Now slowly bring your finger close to a water tap. See the spark fly. You have just given yourself a shock!

What just happened?

You acted as a conductor of electricity when your back was rubbed. The glass you were standing on, however, kept you insulated and prevented the harmful effects of the shock.

The Tissue Dance

Duration of Experiment: 20 mins.

Difficulty Level:

What you need:

Tissue paper

Glass pane

Two thick books

Woollen fabric

What to do:

Step 1. Place the glass pane across two thick books.

Step 2. Tear the tissue into small pieces and put it under the glass.

Step 3. Rub the glass with the wool.

Step 4. Watch the tissue jump up and dance.

What just happened?

Rubbing the glass produced static electricity to which, the tissue pieces were attracted.

Jumping Pepper

Duration of Experiment: 10 mins.

Difficulty Level:

What you need:

Pepper

Woollen fabric

Plastic box

What to do:

Step 1. Sprinkle a thin layer of pepper into a small plastic box.

Step 2. Shut the box and rub the lid with the woollen fabric.

Step 3. See the pepper jump up and stick to the lid.

What just happened?

Rubbing the lid of the box caused a build-up of static electricity to which the pepper was attracted.

Salt and Pepper Separation

Duration of Experiment: 10 mins.

Difficulty Level:

What you need:

Salt

Pepper

Plastic spoon

Woollen fabric

What to do:

Step 1. Sprinkle a little salt and pepper on a flat surface and mix them up.

Step 2. Rub a plastic spoon with the wool.

Step 3. Hold the spoon above the salt and pepper, and bring it down slowly.

Step 4. The pepper particles will jump up and stick to the spoon.

What just happened?

When you charge the spoon, the salt and the pepper become attracted to it. However, because pepper is lighter than salt, it jumps up before the salt.

Combing Sparks

Duration of Experiment: 10 mins.

Difficulty Level:

What you need:

Comb

Metal doorknob

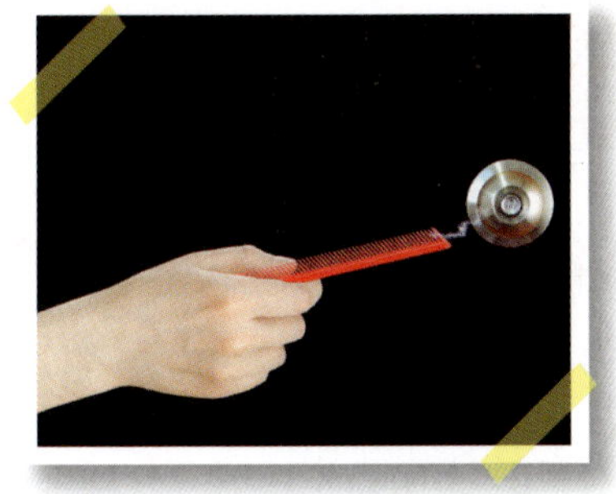

What to do:

Step 1. On a dry day, comb your hair briskly to 'charge' the comb.

Step 2. Hold the end of the comb about half a centimetre above the doorknob in a dark room.

Step 3. You will see a tiny spark jump across.

What just happened?

Combing your hair creates static electricity which gives rise to the sparks.

Create Static

Duration of Experiment: 15 mins.

Difficulty Level:

What you need:

Nail

Metal jar cover

Wooden ruler

Woollen fabric

Phonograph record

What to do:

Step 1. Nail the metal cover to the ruler.

Step 2. Rub the record with the wool for 15 seconds.

Step 3. Holding the ruler, touch the metal cover to the record.

Step 4. Touch the metal cover and the record simultaneously with your free hand.

Step 5. You will observe a spark jump.

What just happened?

Rubbing the record created a charge in the record. This electric charge gave off the spark when you touched it.

Static Flower

Duration of Experiment: 10 mins.

Difficulty Level:

What you need:

Pencil

Tape

Scissors

Wire

Tissue paper

Balloon

What to do:

Step 1. Make small loops at both ends of the wire.

Step 2. Cut thin strips out of the tissue paper and push them in through one end such that equal lengths of paper stick out.

Step 3. Tape the pencil to the middle of the wire to make a handle.

Step 4. Blow up the balloon and rub it in your hair to create static.

Step 5. Hold the pencil in your hand and touch the balloon to the free end of the wire.

Step 6. Watch the 'petals' unfold.

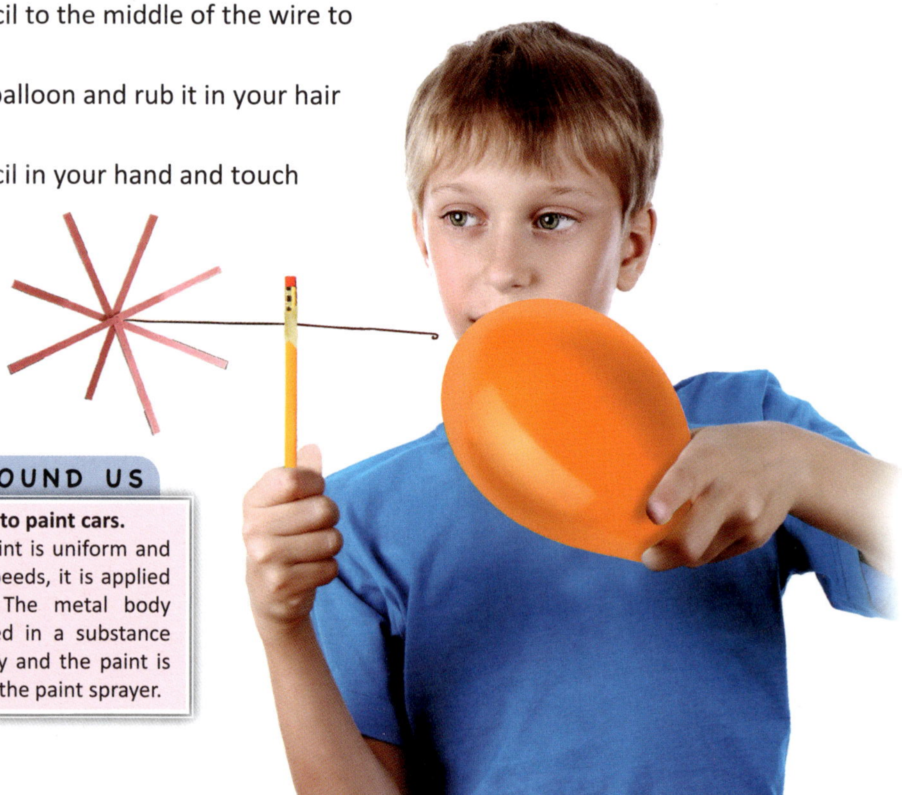

SCIENCE AROUND US

Static electricity is used to paint cars.
To make sure a car's paint is uniform and that it will resist high speeds, it is applied with a static charge. The metal body of the car is submerged in a substance that charges it positively and the paint is charged negatively with the paint sprayer.

What just happened?

The balloon transfers its charge through the wire to the paper petals. Having the same charge, the petals repel each other and stick out in different directions.

Bubble Ballet

Duration of Experiment: 15 mins.

Difficulty Level:

What you need:

Comb

Bubble liquid

Wire

Stool

What to do:

Step 1. Twist the wire to form the shape of a bubble blower.
Step 2. Blow some bubbles onto a flat surface, like a stool.
Step 3. Run the comb through your hair and hold it close to some bubbles.
Step 4. The bubbles, attracted to the comb, form interesting shapes.

What just happened?

The charged comb attracts the bubbles towards it, making them change their shape.

Merry-go-round

Duration of Experiment: 15 mins.

Difficulty Level:

What you need:

Cork

Scissors

Glass

Paper

Needle

Woollen fabric

What to do:

Step 1. Cut out a cross from the paper.
Step 2. Push a needle into the cork. Balance the cross on top of the needle. Turn the glass over this.
Step 3. Rub the glass with the woollen fabric and see the cross rotate.

What just happened?

By rubbing the glass, you created a negative charge. Repelled by this, the paper rotates.

Electrical Paper Hanging

Duration of Experiment: 15 mins.

Difficulty Level:

What you need:

Paper

Long wooden ruler

Chair

What to do:

Step 1. Balance the ruler on the top of the chair.

Step 2. Rub the paper in your hair and then hold the paper just below the ruler.

Step 3. The ruler tips over without you touching it.

What just happened? The paper got electrically charged when you rubbed it in your hair. When you held it near the ruler, it got attracted to the paper and tipped over.

Electric Pendulum

Duration of Experiment: 15 mins.

Difficulty Level:

What you need:

Copper wire

Corks

String

Comb

Glass bottle

What to do:

Step 1. Shut the bottle with the cork.

Step 2. Stick the wire into the cork, parallel to the ground.

Step 3. Tie the string to the end of the wire.

Step 4. Tie a small piece of cork to the bottom of the string.

Step 5. Run the comb through your hair and hold it close to the cork. Enjoy your swinging pendulum.

What just happened?

The comb got electrically charged when you combed your hair and attracted the small cork towards it.

Magic Wand

Duration of Experiment: 15 mins.

Difficulty Level:

What you need:

Pencil

PVC pipe

Scissors

Tape

Styrofoam sheets

Woollen fabric

What to do:

Step 1. Cut out a strip from the styrofoam sheet.
Step 2. Tape the ends together to make a ring.
Step 3. Rub the woolen fabric on the ring.
Step 4. Tape the pencil to the end of the PVC pipe.
Step 5. Use the pencil and pipe to toss the ring up in the air.
Step 6. Quickly position the pipe under the ring to make it levitate!

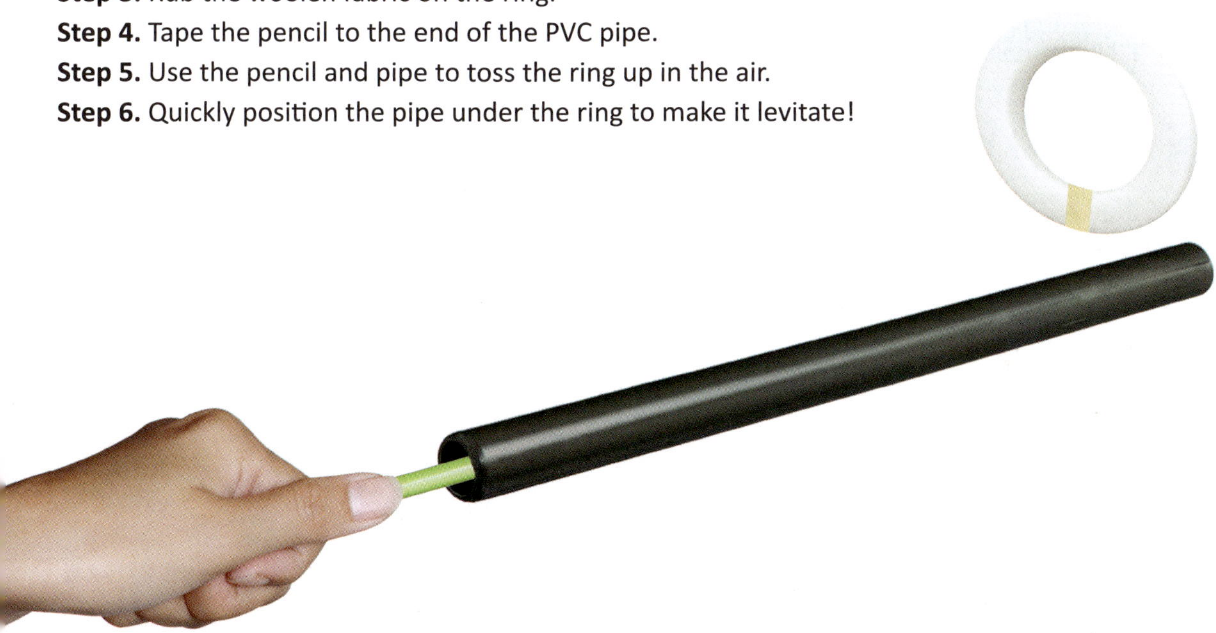

What just happened? The static charge in the pipe repelled the charge in the styrofoam ring.

Balloon Attraction

Duration of Experiment: 10 mins.

Difficulty Level:

What you need:

2 balloons

String

Woollen fabric

What to do:

Step 1. Blow up two balloons and tie strings to them.

Step 2. Hold the balloons from the strings about 3 cm apart.

Step 3. Rub one balloon against the woollen fabric.

Step 4. Watch as the balloons get attracted to each other.

Step 5. Now rub the other balloon to the woollen fabric as well.

Step 6. Notice how they repel each other.

What just happened?

Before rubbing the fabric both balloons had neutral charges and were neither attracted to nor repelled by each other. When you rubbed only one balloon, it got charged. The second balloon, however, was still neutral, so they were attracted to each other. However, when both balloons were rubbed, both of them got charged and repelled each other.

Genie in a Bottle

Duration of Experiment: 15 mins.

Difficulty Level:

What you need:

Styrofoam beads

Plastic bottle

What to do:

Step 1. Fill half the bottle with the styrofoam beads.

Step 2. Rub the bottle to your hair.

Step 3. Run your hand over the bottle to see the beads jumping to avoid your finger.

What just happened?

When you rubbed the bottle to your hair, it created an electric charge. This charge got transferred to the styrofoam. Your hand too, has a similar charge, which causes the styrofoam to get repelled by your hand.

Holy Balloon!

Duration of Experiment: 15 mins.

Difficulty Level:

What you need:

Scissors

Woollen fabric

Balloon

Plastic bag

What to do:

Step 1. Cut out a strip from the open end of the plastic bag.

Step 2. Blow the balloon and tie it up.

Step 3. Rub the balloon with the woollen fabric for 45 seconds.

Step 4. Flatten the plastic ring and rub it with the same woollen fabric.

Step 5. Leave the band about one foot over the balloon and release it.

The ring floats over the balloon, giving it a halo!

What just happened?

Rubbing the plastic and the balloon gives them both the same charge, which makes them repel each other.

Spinning Matchsticks

Duration of Experiment: 15 mins.

Difficulty Level:

What you need:

2 copper coins

Matchsticks

Plastic cup

Balloon

What to do:

Step 1. Balance one coin vertically on the base of the other.

Step 2. Balance the matchstick horizontally on this.

Step 3. Carefully put the plastic cup over this apparatus.

Step 4. Blow up the balloon and tie it.

Step 5. Rub the balloon against your hair and bring it near the glass.

Step 6. Watch as the matchstick follows the balloon.

What just happened?

Rubbing the balloon created a negative charge in the balloon. The matchstick has a neutral charge and was attracted to the balloon, which is why it 'followed' the balloon.

Making Lightning

Duration of Experiment: 10 mins.

Difficulty Level:

What you need:

Balloon

Sweater

Metal surface

What to do:

Step 1. Blow the balloon and go in a dark room.

Step 2. Rub the balloon vigorously against the sweater.

Step 3. Move the balloon close to the metal surface.

Step 4. There will be a spark between the balloon and the metal.

What just happened?

The balloon is being used to create static electricity. The flash or spark that jumps from the balloon to the metal object is like lightning, though much smaller in scale.

Illuminating Balloon

Duration of Experiment: 10 mins.

Difficulty Level:

What you need:

Bulb

Balloon

What to do:

Step 1. In a dark room, rub the balloon to your hair for five minutes.

Step 2. Touch it to the light bulb.

Step 3. You will be able to see sparks.

What just happened? When the charged balloon touched the bulb, electrons passed from the balloon to the bulb, causing it to emit small sparks of light.

Light It

Duration of Experiment: 10 mins.

Difficulty Level:

What you need:

Tubelight

Balloon

What to do:

Step 1. Blow the balloon.

Step 2. Go to a dark room.

Step 3. Rub the tube light with the balloon.

Step 4. Hold the balloon to the end of the tube light.

Step 5. It will light up.

What just happened?

The ends of the tube light are sensitive to electric currents. As soon as it comes in contact with the balloon which you charged by rubbing, it lights up.

Electroscope

Duration of Experiment: 15 mins.

Difficulty Level:

What you need:

Comb

Aluminium plate

Copper wire

Aluminium foil

Glass jar

What to do:

Step 1. Bend the copper wire in a 'Z' shape.
Step 2. Fold the foil and hang it on the bottom of the wire.
Step 3. Leave the top horizontal part over the top of the jar.
Step 4. Put the aluminium plate on top to hold it in place.
Step 5. Run the comb through your hair and bring it close to the jar.
Step 6. You will see the two strips of aluminium spring apart.

What just happened?

When you bring the comb close to the aluminium foil, it becomes charged. Since like charges repel, the aluminium foil leaves repel each other.

Jumpy Beads

Duration of Experiment: 10 mins.

Difficulty Level:

What you need:

Styrofoam balls

Balloon

What to do:

Step 1. Fill the balloon with styrofoam balls.

Step 2. Inflate the balloon and tie it.

Step 3. Rub the balloon to your hair.

Step 4. Watch the balls in the balloon jump around!

What just happened? As the static electricity charged the balloon, the styrofoam balls too were attracted, then repelled by the walls of the balloon, causing them to jump around.

Static Ghost

Duration of Experiment: 20 mins.

Difficulty Level:

What you need:

2 books

Glycerine

Paintbrush

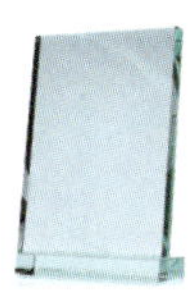

Glass pane

Tissue paper

Woollen fabric

What to do:

Step 1. Paint a face on the glass pane using glycerine.

Step 2. Place the glass, with the glycerine painted side facing down, an inch above with the help of the books.

Step 3. Finely shred the tissue. Put it under the glass.

Step 4. Rub the glass with the woollen fabric.

See your invisible face come into sight!

What just happened?

The static caused the paper to stick to the glass. The glycerine allowed the paper to stay stuck.

Glowing Sugar

Duration of Experiment: 15 mins.

Difficulty Level:

What you need:

Sugar lumps

Pliers

What to do:

Step 1. Take the sugar lumps to a dark room.

Step 2. Crush them with the pliers.

Step 3. You will be able to see small flashes of blue-green sparks.

What just happened?

When sugar crystals break, sometimes, one side has more positive charge that the other. When you crush the lumps, you are pulling apart the positive and the negative charges. This gives off enough energy to make it spark.

Musical Glasses

Duration of Experiment: 20 mins.

Difficulty Level:

What you need:

Pencil

Glasses

Water

What to do:

Step 1. Put all the glasses in a line. Fill the first one with a little water, the second with slightly more and so on.

Step 2. Hit the rim of the glass with the least amount of water using a pencil and observe the sound. Then, hit the rim of glass with the most water. Notice the difference in the sound.

Step 3. Enjoy creating a tune!

What just happened?

Small vibrations are made when you hit the glass. This creates sound waves which travel through the water. More water means slower vibrations and a deeper tone.

Jumping Rice

Duration of Experiment: 10 mins.

Difficulty Level:

What you need:

Rice

Bowl

Pan

Spoon

Cling wrap

Rubber bands

What to do:

Step 1. Stretch the cling wrap over the top of the bowl and secure it with a rubber band.

Step 2. Sprinkle a few grains of rice on top.

Step 3. Hold the pan close to the bowl and hit it with the spoon to see the rice jump!

What just happened?

Sound travels in the form of waves. The waves travel through the air and hit the cling wrap, making it vibrate. The vibrations cause the rice to jump.

The Spoon Bell

Duration of Experiment: 5 mins.

Difficulty Level:

What you need:

Scissors

String

Metal spoon

Table

What to do:

Step 1. Tie the spoon in the middle with the string.

Step 2. Hold one end of the thread to your right ear and the other to your left ear.

Step 3. Walk to the table and swing slowly so that the spoon gently bangs against the edge of the table. It will sound like a bell.

What just happened?

The metal begins to vibrate when you bang it against the table. These vibrations are carried by the strings straight up to your ears.

The Clucking Cup

Duration of Experiment: 15 mins.

Difficulty Level:

What you need:

Plastic cup

String

Paper clip

Paper towel

Scissors

Water

What to do:

Step 1. Make a hole in the centre of the base of the cup.

Step 2. Tie one end of the string to the middle of the paper clip.

Step 3. Push the other end of the string through the hole in the cup.

Step 4. Hold the cup upside down in one hand.

Step 5. Wet a paper towel and fold it.

Step 6. Wrap the paper towel around the string and tug on it in short jerks.

Step 7. The sound you create is a lot like a clucking hen!

SCIENCE AROUND US

What causes echoes?

An echo occurs when a sound wave bounces off a surface and arrives at the listener some time after the direct sound. Echoes can be very useful in finding out the depth of the ocean and finding things lost at sea.

What just happened?

Tugging on the string makes it vibrate, creating a sound. The shape of the cup amplifies this sound, giving rise to the fascinating sound.

Dancing Dolls

Duration of Experiment: 15 mins.

Difficulty Level:

What you need:

Glass pane

Scissors

Tissue paper

Table

Two thick books

Flannel cloth

What to do:

Step 1. Cut out two figures in the shape of dolls using the tissue paper.

Step 2. Put the two books on a table and put the glass pane on top of it.

Step 3. Put the two dolls below the glass between the two books.

Step 4. Rub the glass with the flannel cloth and watch your dolls dance.

What just happened?

The charged glass attracts the dolls, so they stand up. When they touch the glass, they become charged and are repelled. So, they lay back down.

Fruit Battery

Duration of Experiment: 15 mins.

Difficulty Level:

What you need:

Electric tape

Copper nails

Lime

Small light bulb

Wire

What to do:

Step 1. Squeeze the lime without breaking its skin.

Step 2. Insert both nails into the fruit at a distance of 2 inches from each other.

Step 3. Peel the plastic insulation off the bulb (leads of the light).

Step 4. Wrap the wires around the head of the two nails.

Step 5. Secure the wire around the nails using electric tape.

What just happened?

Citric fruits conduct electricity because of their acidic content. The different charges of the lime and the nail causes the electric flow.

Waterproof Bag

Duration of Experiment: 10 mins.

Difficulty Level:

What you need:

Sharp pencils

Ziplock bag

Water

What to do:

Step 1. Fill half the ziplock bag with water and seal it.

Step 2. Push the pencils through the bag.

Step 3. Push as many pencils as you like, the water will not leak out of the bag!

What just happened?

Plastic is a polymer. This means that it is made up of small, chain–like molecules. These molecules wrap themselves around the pencil, sealing it.

The Mysterious Portrait

Duration of Experiment: 10 mins.

Difficulty Level:

What you need:

Pencil

Battery

Iron fillings

3 cardboard sheets

Wire

Scissors

Glue

What to do:

Step 1. Draw a face on one of the cardboard sheets. Cut it out.

Step 2. Paste this on another cardboard sheet.

Step 3. Stick the wire on the outline of the face.

Step 4. Paste the last cardboard sheet on top of on the first one to conceal the face.

Step 5. Sprinkle iron fillings on the cardboard and connect the wire to the battery.

Step 6. Tap the cardboard and watch the fillings magically form a face.

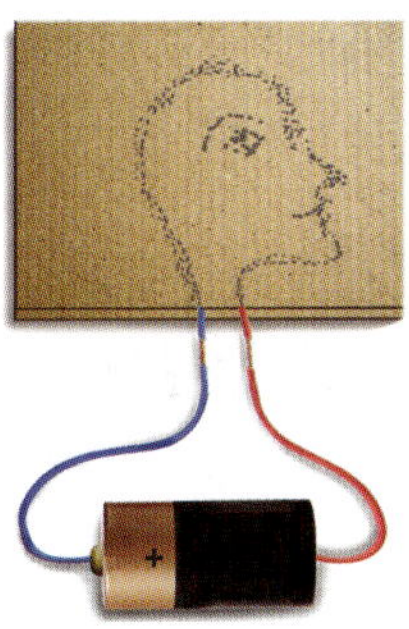

What just happened?

By connecting the wire to a battery, the electric circuit was complete. This created a magnetic field around the wire, which means that the wire begins to act as a magnet. This attracts the iron fillings and they create a face.

OTHER TITLES IN THIS SERIES

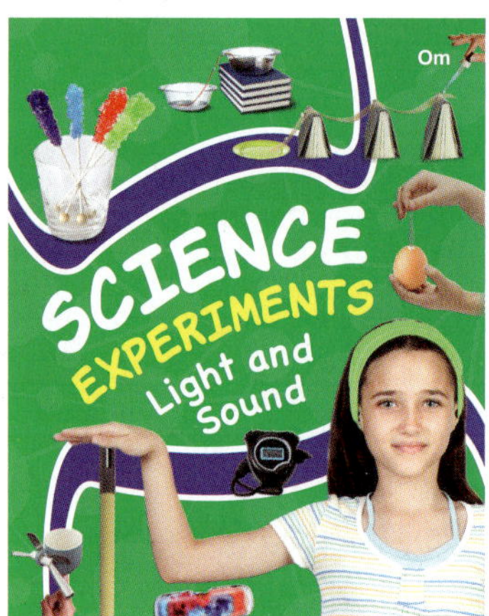